Intentionally Positive

Live to inspire the next generation.

— Shani T Night

Hardcover ISBN: 978-1-953364-31-9
Paperback ISBN: 978-1-953364-30-2

Infinite Generations
137 National Plaza, STE 300
National Harbor, MD 20745

Printed in the United States of America

First Printing, 2022

Art by Canva
Cover Design by: I Howard

Positive Media, Happy Life
www.InfiniteGenerations.com

Intentionally Positive

Taking the time to put you first.

- Shani T. Night

Dear Reader:

Thank you for your purchase.
I hope you enjoy Intentionally Positive Planner.

Please share a review of this planner on Amazon.

Visit my website for discounts, contests, and/or giveaways.
www.shanitnight.com

Follow Shani Night:
instagram.com/shaninight
www.facebook.com/ShaniTNight
I post daily/weekly positive messages.

"Be fearless and life will be limitless. You'll inspire someone along the way."

Shani T. Night

Intentionally Positive

This planner was created based on what I've done to live a more positive and inspired life, which I believe has led to me living out my dreams—starting with my first quote.

"I aspire to be the best part of me."
- Shani T. Night

This quote led me to more quotes and affirmations that would help change my life and thoughts. There are many steps I've taken, which I share in this book.

I should be honest, I've never been a negative person, but sometimes life and the people in your life have a way of changing that. I genuinely believe that you always find your way back to the true you. But, of course, you now have to live that truth, which leads me to my latest quote.

"Walking in your truth is brave, and shining in your purpose is divine."
- Shani T. Night

Let's continue the journey together!

- Shani J. Night

Intentionally Positive

THIS PLANNER BELONGS TO

YOU MUST START THE JOURNEY
TO FIND YOU

20____ Calendar

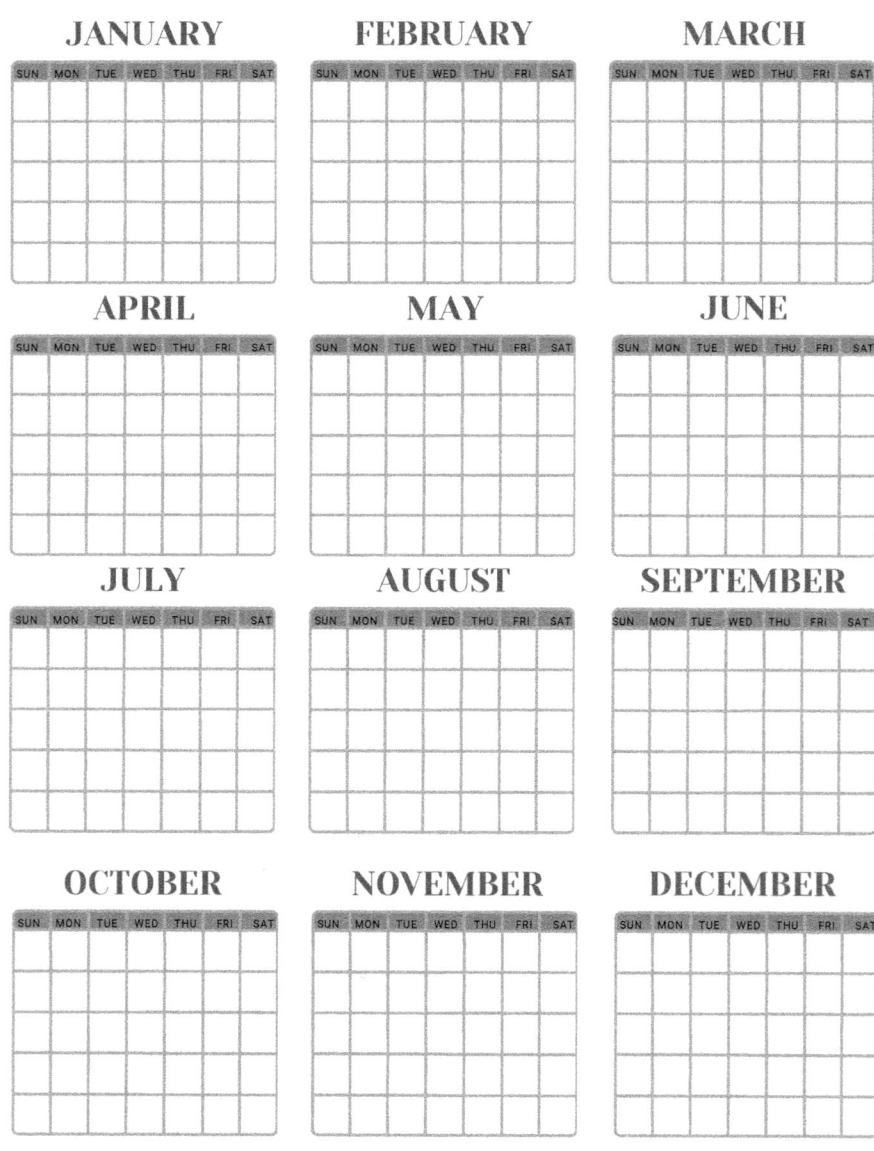

JANUARY

SUN	MON	TUE	WED	THU	FRI	SAT

FEBRUARY

SUN	MON	TUE	WED	THU	FRI	SAT

MARCH

SUN	MON	TUE	WED	THU	FRI	SAT

APRIL

SUN	MON	TUE	WED	THU	FRI	SAT

MAY

SUN	MON	TUE	WED	THU	FRI	SAT

JUNE

SUN	MON	TUE	WED	THU	FRI	SAT

JULY

SUN	MON	TUE	WED	THU	FRI	SAT

AUGUST

SUN	MON	TUE	WED	THU	FRI	SAT

SEPTEMBER

SUN	MON	TUE	WED	THU	FRI	SAT

OCTOBER

SUN	MON	TUE	WED	THU	FRI	SAT

NOVEMBER

SUN	MON	TUE	WED	THU	FRI	SAT

DECEMBER

SUN	MON	TUE	WED	THU	FRI	SAT

YEARLY PLANNER

January

February

March

April

May

June

July

August

September

October

November

December

I am the designer of my life; I build my foundation positively and choose its contents wisely.

Shani T. Night

Important Dates

DATE	EVENT	NOTES

"The road less traveled can lead to marvelous things."

You got this!

Shani T. Night

Good Morning Sunshine

(I always welcome sunshine into my day, first thing in the morning: so welcome sunshine and an open heart to declutter your mind. Continue to do this each day. Share thoughts on how you feel about doing this below.)

Monthly
DECLUTTER YOUR MIND

SET ASPIRATIONS

Think about your aspirations and write them down. Aspirations are more future-focused, like your dreams, hopes, and ambitions.

IDENTIFY YOUR ANEW

Is there anything you did not get accomplished that you set out for yesterday, last week, last month, or last year?

RECOGNIZE - YOU NEED PEACE

Let go of what is not allowing you to have peace. Identify those things and then identify what brings you peace.

SET GOALS

If you don't have a list, identify one goal. Remember, goals are more short-term focused and usually have actions that follow them.

IDENTIFY YOUR INTENTIONS

Are your intentions to be kind and loving?

WELCOME CHANGE - IDENTIFY WHAT YOU CAN DO BETTER

Identify what you need to change in your life or what you want to change.

GRATITUDE REFLECTION - WHAT ARE YOU GRATEFUL FOR AND WHY?

Write it down and reflect on why you feel grateful.

Positive Thoughts

(Thinking positive starts with you; identify what makes you happy and stay positive.)

Weekly Intentions

IDENTIFY YOUR INTENTIONS FOR THE WEEK.

CHANGE
Change is hard, and recognizing change and implementing it is even more challenging, but if you stay positive and focus on being a better you, it will pay off.

ELIMINATE NEGATIVITY AROUND YOU
people/habits/interactions

IDENTIFY WHAT YOU NEED TO WORK ON
Is there anything you did not get accomplished?

LIST THREE THINGS YOU ARE GRATEFUL FOR.
They can be big or small, specific or general. Focus on the positive feelings associated with each. Approach the gratitude exercise with intention.

WELCOME POSITIVE THOUGHTS
Don't forget to welcome sunshine into your day first thing in the morning: welcome sunshine and an open heart to declutter your mind. Continue to do this each day. Share thoughts on how you feel about doing this on the next page.

Intentionally Positive

Positive Thoughts

(Thinking positive starts with you; identify what makes you happy and stay positive.)

WEEKLY PLANNER

MONDAY

TUESDAY

WEDNESDAY

THURSDAY

FRIDAY

SATURDAY

SUNDAY

WEEK OF _____

GOALS

TO DO LIST

PRIORITIES

WEEKLY PLANNER

Monday

Tuesday

Wednesday

Thursday

Friday

Saturday/Sunday

Weekly Notes

to do today

DATE _____

1 _____ ☐

2 _____ ☐

3 _____ ☐

4 _____ ☐

5 _____ ☐

6 _____ ☐

7 _____ ☐

8 _____ ☐

9 _____ ☐

10 _____ ☐

note for today

Weekly Successes

IDENTIFY WHAT SUCCESS LOOKS LIKE TO YOU AND YOU ALONE. **(Don't try to match someone else's success)**

REFLECT

RECOGNIZE THE POSITIVE STEPS YOU'VE TAKEN THIS WEEK TO BE POSITIVE AND DECLUTTER YOUR MIND. **(Take a moment to applaud yourself for taking the necessary steps to start a more positive life.)**

LIST ONE NEGATIVE THING YOU DISCOVERED AROUND YOU. **(people/habits/interactions)** WHAT DID YOU DO ABOUT IT?

WHAT DID YOU DISCOVER ABOUT YOURSELF THIS WEEK?

DID YOU WELCOME CHANGE? WHAT DID YOU CHANGE?

WHAT ARE THREE RECENT ACCOMPLISHMENTS THAT YOU ARE PROUD OF, AND WHAT LESSONS DID YOU DISCOVER IN THE PROCESS?

Intentionally Positive

Weekly Takeaways

NOTE TO SELF

I move impediments out of
my way; my future is carved
towards greatness.

Shani T. Night

Good Morning Sunshine

(I always welcome sunshine into my day, first thing in the morning: so welcome sunshine and an open heart to declutter your mind. Continue to do this each day. Share thoughts on how you feel about doing this below.)

Weekly Intentions

IDENTIFY YOUR INTENTIONS FOR THE WEEK.

CHANGE
Change is hard, and recognizing change and implementing it is even more challenging, but if you stay positive and focus on being a better you, it will pay off.

ELIMINATE NEGATIVITY AROUND YOU
people/habits/interactions

IDENTIFY WHAT YOU NEED TO WORK ON
Is there anything you did not get accomplished?

LIST THREE THINGS YOU ARE GRATEFUL FOR.
They can be big or small, specific or general. Focus on the positive feelings associated with each. Approach the gratitude exercise with intention.

WELCOME POSITIVE THOUGHTS
Don't forget to welcome sunshine into your day first thing in the morning: welcome sunshine and an open heart to declutter your mind. Continue to do this each day. Share thoughts on how you feel about doing this on the next page.

Intentionally Positive

Positive Thoughts

(Thinking positive starts with you; identify what makes you happy and stay positive.)

WEEKLY PLANNER

MONDAY

TUESDAY

WEDNESDAY

THURSDAY

FRIDAY

SATURDAY

SUNDAY

WEEK OF _____

GOALS

_____
_____
_____
_____
_____

TO DO LIST

_____
_____
_____
_____
_____
_____
_____
_____
_____

PRIORITIES

WEEKLY PLANNER

Monday

Tuesday

Wednesday

Thursday

Friday

Saturday/Sunday

Weekly Notes

to do today

DATE ....

1 _____ ☐

2 _____ ☐

3 _____ ☐

4 _____ ☐

5 _____ ☐

6 _____ ☐

7 _____ ☐

8 _____ ☐

9 _____ ☐

10 _____ ☐

note for today

Weekly Successes

IDENTIFY WHAT SUCCESS LOOKS LIKE TO YOU AND YOU ALONE. **(Don't try to match someone else's success)**

REFLECT

RECOGNIZE THE POSITIVE STEPS YOU'VE TAKEN THIS WEEK TO BE POSITIVE AND DECLUTTER YOUR MIND. **(Take a moment to applaud yourself for taking the necessary steps to start a more positive life.)**

LIST ONE NEGATIVE THING YOU DISCOVERED AROUND YOU. **(people/habits/interactions)** WHAT DID YOU DO ABOUT IT?

WHAT DID YOU DISCOVER ABOUT YOURSELF THIS WEEK?

DID YOU WELCOME CHANGE? WHAT DID YOU CHANGE?

WHAT ARE THREE RECENT ACCOMPLISHMENTS THAT YOU ARE PROUD OF, AND WHAT LESSONS DID YOU DISCOVER IN THE PROCESS?

Weekly Takeaways

NOTE TO SELF

Positive energy surges through me and leads me to brilliant things.

- Shani J. Night

Good Morning Sunshine

(I always welcome sunshine into my day, first thing in the morning: so welcome sunshine and an open heart to declutter your mind. Continue to do this each day. Share thoughts on how you feel about doing this below.)

Weekly Intentions

IDENTIFY YOUR INTENTIONS FOR THE WEEK.

CHANGE

Change is hard, and recognizing change and implementing it is even more challenging, but if you stay positive and focus on being a better you, it will pay off.

ELIMINATE NEGATIVITY AROUND YOU

people/habits/interactions

IDENTIFY WHAT YOU NEED TO WORK ON

Is there anything you did not get accomplished?

LIST THREE THINGS YOU ARE GRATEFUL FOR.

They can be big or small, specific or general. Focus on the positive feelings associated with each. Approach the gratitude exercise with intention.

WELCOME POSITIVE THOUGHTS

Don't forget to welcome sunshine into your day first thing in the morning: welcome sunshine and an open heart to declutter your mind. Continue to do this each day. Share thoughts on how you feel about doing this on the next page.

Intentionally Positive

Positive Thoughts

(Thinking positive starts with you; identify what makes you happy and stay positive.)

WEEKLY PLANNER

WEEK OF _____

MONDAY

TUESDAY

WEDNESDAY

THURSDAY

FRIDAY

SATURDAY

SUNDAY

GOALS

_____

_____

_____

_____

_____

TO DO LIST

_____

_____

_____

_____

_____

_____

_____

_____

PRIORITIES

WEEKLY PLANNER

Monday

Tuesday

Wednesday

Thursday

Friday

Saturday/Sunday

Weekly Notes

to do today

DATE ....

1 _____ ☐

2 _____ ☐

3 _____ ☐

4 _____ ☐

5 _____ ☐

6 _____ ☐

7 _____ ☐

8 _____ ☐

9 _____ ☐

10 _____ ☐

note for today

Weekly Successes

IDENTIFY WHAT SUCCESS LOOKS LIKE TO YOU AND YOU ALONE. **(Don't try to match someone else's success)**

REFLECT

RECOGNIZE THE POSITIVE STEPS YOU'VE TAKEN THIS WEEK TO BE POSITIVE AND DECLUTTER YOUR MIND. **(Take a moment to applaud yourself for taking the necessary steps to start a more positive life.)**

LIST ONE NEGATIVE THING YOU DISCOVERED AROUND YOU. **(people/habits/interactions)** WHAT DID YOU DO ABOUT IT?

WHAT DID YOU DISCOVER ABOUT YOURSELF THIS WEEK?

DID YOU WELCOME CHANGE? WHAT DID YOU CHANGE?

WHAT ARE THREE RECENT ACCOMPLISHMENTS THAT YOU ARE PROUD OF, AND WHAT LESSONS DID YOU DISCOVER IN THE PROCESS?

Weekly Takeaways

NOTE TO SELF

> **"**
>
> Inspiration surges through me
> and leads me to new ideas.
>
> *Shani T. Night*

Good Morning Sunshine

(I always welcome sunshine into my day, first thing in the morning: so welcome sunshine and an open heart to declutter your mind. Continue to do this each day. Share thoughts on how you feel about doing this below.)

Weekly Intentions

IDENTIFY YOUR INTENTIONS FOR THE WEEK.

CHANGE

Change is hard, and recognizing change and implementing it is even more challenging, but if you stay positive and focus on being a better you, it will pay off.

ELIMINATE NEGATIVITY AROUND YOU

people/habits/interactions

IDENTIFY WHAT YOU NEED TO WORK ON

Is there anything you did not get accomplished?

LIST THREE THINGS YOU ARE GRATEFUL FOR.

They can be big or small, specific or general. Focus on the positive feelings associated with each. Approach the gratitude exercise with intention.

WELCOME POSITIVE THOUGHTS

Don't forget to welcome sunshine into your day first thing in the morning: welcome sunshine and an open heart to declutter your mind. Continue to do this each day. Share thoughts on how you feel about doing this on the next page.

Intentionally Positive

Positive Thoughts

(Thinking positive starts with you; identify what makes you happy and stay positive.)

WEEKLY PLANNER

WEEK OF _____

MONDAY

TUESDAY

WEDNESDAY

THURSDAY

FRIDAY

SATURDAY

SUNDAY

GOALS

TO DO LIST

PRIORITIES

WEEKLY PLANNER

Monday

Tuesday

Wednesday

Thursday

Friday

Saturday/Sunday

Weekly Notes

to do today

DATE

1. _____ ☐
2. _____ ☐
3. _____ ☐
4. _____ ☐
5. _____ ☐
6. _____ ☐
7. _____ ☐
8. _____ ☐
9. _____ ☐
10. _____ ☐

note for today

Weekly Successes

IDENTIFY WHAT SUCCESS LOOKS LIKE TO YOU AND YOU ALONE. **(Don't try to match someone else's success)**

REFLECT

RECOGNIZE THE POSITIVE STEPS YOU'VE TAKEN THIS WEEK TO BE POSITIVE AND DECLUTTER YOUR MIND. **(Take a moment to applaud yourself for taking the necessary steps to start a more positive life.)**

LIST ONE NEGATIVE THING YOU DISCOVERED AROUND YOU. **(people/habits/interactions)** WHAT DID YOU DO ABOUT IT?

WHAT DID YOU DISCOVER ABOUT YOURSELF THIS WEEK?

DID YOU WELCOME CHANGE? WHAT DID YOU CHANGE?

WHAT ARE THREE RECENT ACCOMPLISHMENTS THAT YOU ARE PROUD OF, AND WHAT LESSONS DID YOU DISCOVER IN THE PROCESS?

Intentionally Positive

Weekly Takeaways

NOTE TO SELF

Next Month

"There is always time for growth, new thoughts, and a new direction. Life is evolving."

WELCOMING THE NEXT MONTH WITH OPEN ARMS!

— Shani J. Night

Next Steps

> **"**
>
> I wake up today with love in my heart, strength in my soul, and clarity in my mind.
>
> *Shani T. Night*

Good Morning Sunshine

(I always welcome sunshine into my day, first thing in the morning: so welcome sunshine and an open heart to declutter your mind. Continue to do this each day. Share thoughts on how you feel about doing this below.)

Monthly
DECLUTTER YOUR MIND

SET ASPIRATIONS

Think about your aspirations and write them down. Aspirations are more future-focused, like your dreams, hopes, and ambitions.

IDENTIFY YOUR ANEW

Is there anything you did not get accomplished that you set out for yesterday, last week, last month, or last year?

RECOGNIZE - YOU NEED PEACE

Let go of what is not allowing you to have peace. Identify those things and then identify what brings you peace.

SET GOALS

If you don't have a list, identify one goal. Remember, goals are more short-term focused and usually have actions that follow them.

IDENTIFY YOUR INTENTIONS

Are your intentions to be kind and loving?

WELCOME CHANGE - IDENTIFY WHAT YOU CAN DO BETTER

Identify what you need to change in your life or what you want to change.

GRATITUDE REFLECTION - WHAT ARE YOU GRATEFUL FOR AND WHY?

Write it down and reflect on why you feel grateful.

Positive Thoughts

(Thinking positive starts with you; identify what makes you
happy and stay positive.)

Weekly Intentions

IDENTIFY YOUR INTENTIONS FOR THE WEEK.

CHANGE
Change is hard, and recognizing change and implementing it is even more challenging, but if you stay positive and focus on being a better you, it will pay off.

ELIMINATE NEGATIVITY AROUND YOU
people/habits/interactions

IDENTIFY WHAT YOU NEED TO WORK ON
Is there anything you did not get accomplished?

LIST THREE THINGS YOU ARE GRATEFUL FOR.
They can be big or small, specific or general. Focus on the positive feelings associated with each. Approach the gratitude exercise with intention.

WELCOME POSITIVE THOUGHTS
Don't forget to welcome sunshine into your day first thing in the morning: welcome sunshine and an open heart to declutter your mind. Continue to do this each day. Share thoughts on how you feel about doing this on the next page.

Intentionally Positive

Positive Thoughts

(Thinking positive starts with you; identify what makes you happy and stay positive.)

WEEKLY PLANNER

MONDAY

TUESDAY

WEDNESDAY

THURSDAY

FRIDAY

SATURDAY

SUNDAY

WEEK OF _____

GOALS

TO DO LIST

PRIORITIES

WEEKLY PLANNER

Monday

Tuesday

Wednesday

Thursday

Friday

Saturday/Sunday

Weekly Notes

to do today

DATE ....

1 _____ ☐

2 _____ ☐

3 _____ ☐

4 _____ ☐

5 _____ ☐

6 _____ ☐

7 _____ ☐

8 _____ ☐

9 _____ ☐

10 _____ ☐

note for today

Weekly Successes

IDENTIFY WHAT SUCCESS LOOKS LIKE TO YOU AND YOU ALONE. **(Don't try to match someone else's success)**

REFLECT

RECOGNIZE THE POSITIVE STEPS YOU'VE TAKEN THIS WEEK TO BE POSITIVE AND DECLUTTER YOUR MIND. **(Take a moment to applaud yourself for taking the necessary steps to start a more positive life.)**

LIST ONE NEGATIVE THING YOU DISCOVERED AROUND YOU. **(people/habits/interactions)** WHAT DID YOU DO ABOUT IT?

WHAT DID YOU DISCOVER ABOUT YOURSELF THIS WEEK?

DID YOU WELCOME CHANGE? WHAT DID YOU CHANGE?

WHAT ARE THREE RECENT ACCOMPLISHMENTS THAT YOU ARE PROUD OF, AND WHAT LESSONS DID YOU DISCOVER IN THE PROCESS?

Weekly Takeaways

NOTE TO SELF

"

The universe rewards my efforts, and my dreams manifest into reality.

Shani T. Night

Good Morning Sunshine

(I always welcome sunshine into my day, first thing in the morning: so welcome sunshine and an open heart to declutter your mind. Continue to do this each day. Share thoughts on how you feel about doing this below.)

Weekly Intentions

IDENTIFY YOUR INTENTIONS FOR THE WEEK.

CHANGE

Change is hard, and recognizing change and implementing it is even more challenging, but if you stay positive and focus on being a better you, it will pay off.

ELIMINATE NEGATIVITY AROUND YOU

people/habits/interactions

IDENTIFY WHAT YOU NEED TO WORK ON

Is there anything you did not get accomplished?

LIST THREE THINGS YOU ARE GRATEFUL FOR.

They can be big or small, specific or general. Focus on the positive feelings associated with each. Approach the gratitude exercise with intention.

WELCOME POSITIVE THOUGHTS

Don't forget to welcome sunshine into your day first thing in the morning: welcome sunshine and an open heart to declutter your mind. Continue to do this each day. Share thoughts on how you feel about doing this on the next page.

Intentionally Positive

Positive Thoughts

(Thinking positive starts with you; identify what makes you happy and stay positive.)

WEEKLY PLANNER

MONDAY

TUESDAY

WEDNESDAY

THURSDAY

FRIDAY

SATURDAY

SUNDAY

WEEK OF _____

GOALS

_____
_____
_____
_____
_____

TO DO LIST

_____
_____
_____
_____
_____
_____
_____

PRIORITIES

WEEKLY PLANNER

Monday

Tuesday

Wednesday

Thursday

Friday

Saturday/Sunday

Weekly Notes

to do today

DATE ....

1 _____ ☐

2 _____ ☐

3 _____ ☐

4 _____ ☐

5 _____ ☐

6 _____ ☐

7 _____ ☐

8 _____ ☐

9 _____ ☐

10 _____ ☐

note for today

Weekly Successes

IDENTIFY WHAT SUCCESS LOOKS LIKE TO YOU AND YOU ALONE. **(Don't try to match someone else's success)**

REFLECT

RECOGNIZE THE POSITIVE STEPS YOU'VE TAKEN THIS WEEK TO BE POSITIVE AND DECLUTTER YOUR MIND. **(Take a moment to applaud yourself for taking the necessary steps to start a more positive life.)**

LIST ONE NEGATIVE THING YOU DISCOVERED AROUND YOU. **(people/habits/interactions)** WHAT DID YOU DO ABOUT IT?

WHAT DID YOU DISCOVER ABOUT YOURSELF THIS WEEK?

DID YOU WELCOME CHANGE? WHAT DID YOU CHANGE?

WHAT ARE THREE RECENT ACCOMPLISHMENTS THAT YOU ARE PROUD OF, AND WHAT LESSONS DID YOU DISCOVER IN THE PROCESS?

Intentionally Positive

Weekly Takeaways

NOTE TO SELF

"
My future is the optimistic projection of what I speak into existence now.

— Shani T. Night

Positive Thoughts

(Thinking positive starts with you; identify what makes you happy and stay positive.)

Weekly Intentions

IDENTIFY YOUR INTENTIONS FOR THE WEEK.

CHANGE

Change is hard, and recognizing change and implementing it is even more challenging, but if you stay positive and focus on being a better you, it will pay off.

ELIMINATE NEGATIVITY AROUND YOU

people/habits/interactions

IDENTIFY WHAT YOU NEED TO WORK ON

Is there anything you did not get accomplished?

LIST THREE THINGS YOU ARE GRATEFUL FOR.

They can be big or small, specific or general. Focus on the positive feelings associated with each. Approach the gratitude exercise with intention.

WELCOME POSITIVE THOUGHTS

Don't forget to welcome sunshine into your day first thing in the morning: welcome sunshine and an open heart to declutter your mind. Continue to do this each day. Share thoughts on how you feel about doing this on the next page.

Intentionally Positive

Positive Thoughts

(Thinking positive starts with you; identify what makes you happy and stay positive.)

WEEKLY PLANNER

WEEK OF _____

MONDAY

TUESDAY

WEDNESDAY

THURSDAY

FRIDAY

SATURDAY

SUNDAY

GOALS

_____
_____
_____
_____
_____

TO DO LIST

_____
_____
_____
_____
_____
_____

PRIORITIES

WEEKLY PLANNER

Monday

Tuesday

Wednesday

Thursday

Friday

Saturday/Sunday

Weekly Notes

to do today

DATE ....

1. _____ ☐
2. _____ ☐
3. _____ ☐
4. _____ ☐
5. _____ ☐
6. _____ ☐
7. _____ ☐
8. _____ ☐
9. _____ ☐
10. _____ ☐

note for today

Weekly Successes

IDENTIFY WHAT SUCCESS LOOKS LIKE TO YOU AND YOU ALONE. **(Don't try to match someone else's success)**

REFLECT

RECOGNIZE THE POSITIVE STEPS YOU'VE TAKEN THIS WEEK TO BE POSITIVE AND DECLUTTER YOUR MIND. **(Take a moment to applaud yourself for taking the necessary steps to start a more positive life.)**

LIST ONE NEGATIVE THING YOU DISCOVERED AROUND YOU. **(people/habits/interactions)** WHAT DID YOU DO ABOUT IT?

WHAT DID YOU DISCOVER ABOUT YOURSELF THIS WEEK?

DID YOU WELCOME CHANGE? WHAT DID YOU CHANGE?

WHAT ARE THREE RECENT ACCOMPLISHMENTS THAT YOU ARE PROUD OF, AND WHAT LESSONS DID YOU DISCOVER IN THE PROCESS?

Weekly Takeaways

NOTE TO SELF

"I am fearless, and I stand up for myself."

- Shani T. Night

Positive Thoughts

(Thinking positive starts with you; identify what makes you happy and stay positive.)

Weekly Intentions

IDENTIFY YOUR INTENTIONS FOR THE WEEK.

CHANGE

Change is hard, and recognizing change and implementing it is even more challenging, but if you stay positive and focus on being a better you, it will pay off.

ELIMINATE NEGATIVITY AROUND YOU

people/habits/interactions

IDENTIFY WHAT YOU NEED TO WORK ON

Is there anything you did not get accomplished?

LIST THREE THINGS YOU ARE GRATEFUL FOR.

They can be big or small, specific or general. Focus on the positive feelings associated with each. Approach the gratitude exercise with intention.

WELCOME POSITIVE THOUGHTS

Don't forget to welcome sunshine into your day first thing in the morning: welcome sunshine and an open heart to declutter your mind. Continue to do this each day. Share thoughts on how you feel about doing this on the next page.

Intentionally Positive

Positive Thoughts

(Thinking positive starts with you; identify what makes you happy and stay positive.)

WEEKLY PLANNER

WEEK OF _____

MONDAY

TUESDAY

WEDNESDAY

THURSDAY

FRIDAY

SATURDAY

SUNDAY

GOALS

TO DO LIST

PRIORITIES

WEEKLY PLANNER

Monday

Tuesday

Wednesday

Thursday

Friday

Saturday/Sunday

Weekly Notes

to do today

DATE ....

1 _____ ☐

2 _____ ☐

3 _____ ☐

4 _____ ☐

5 _____ ☐

6 _____ ☐

7 _____ ☐

8 _____ ☐

9 _____ ☐

10 _____ ☐

note for today

Weekly Successes

IDENTIFY WHAT SUCCESS LOOKS LIKE TO YOU AND YOU ALONE. **(Don't try to match someone else's success)**

REFLECT

RECOGNIZE THE POSITIVE STEPS YOU'VE TAKEN THIS WEEK TO BE POSITIVE AND DECLUTTER YOUR MIND. **(Take a moment to applaud yourself for taking the necessary steps to start a more positive life.)**

LIST ONE NEGATIVE THING YOU DISCOVERED AROUND YOU. **(people/habits/interactions)** WHAT DID YOU DO ABOUT IT?

WHAT DID YOU DISCOVER ABOUT YOURSELF THIS WEEK?

DID YOU WELCOME CHANGE? WHAT DID YOU CHANGE?

WHAT ARE THREE RECENT ACCOMPLISHMENTS THAT YOU ARE PROUD OF, AND WHAT LESSONS DID YOU DISCOVER IN THE PROCESS?

Intentionally Positive

Weekly Takeaways

NOTE TO SELF

Intentionally Positive

"Have hope in the future, trust in your dreams, and love for what you do. So keep going, keep trusting in yourself, and keep love in your heart."
— *Shani T. Night*

WELCOMING THE NEXT MONTH WITH OPEN ARMS!

Next Steps

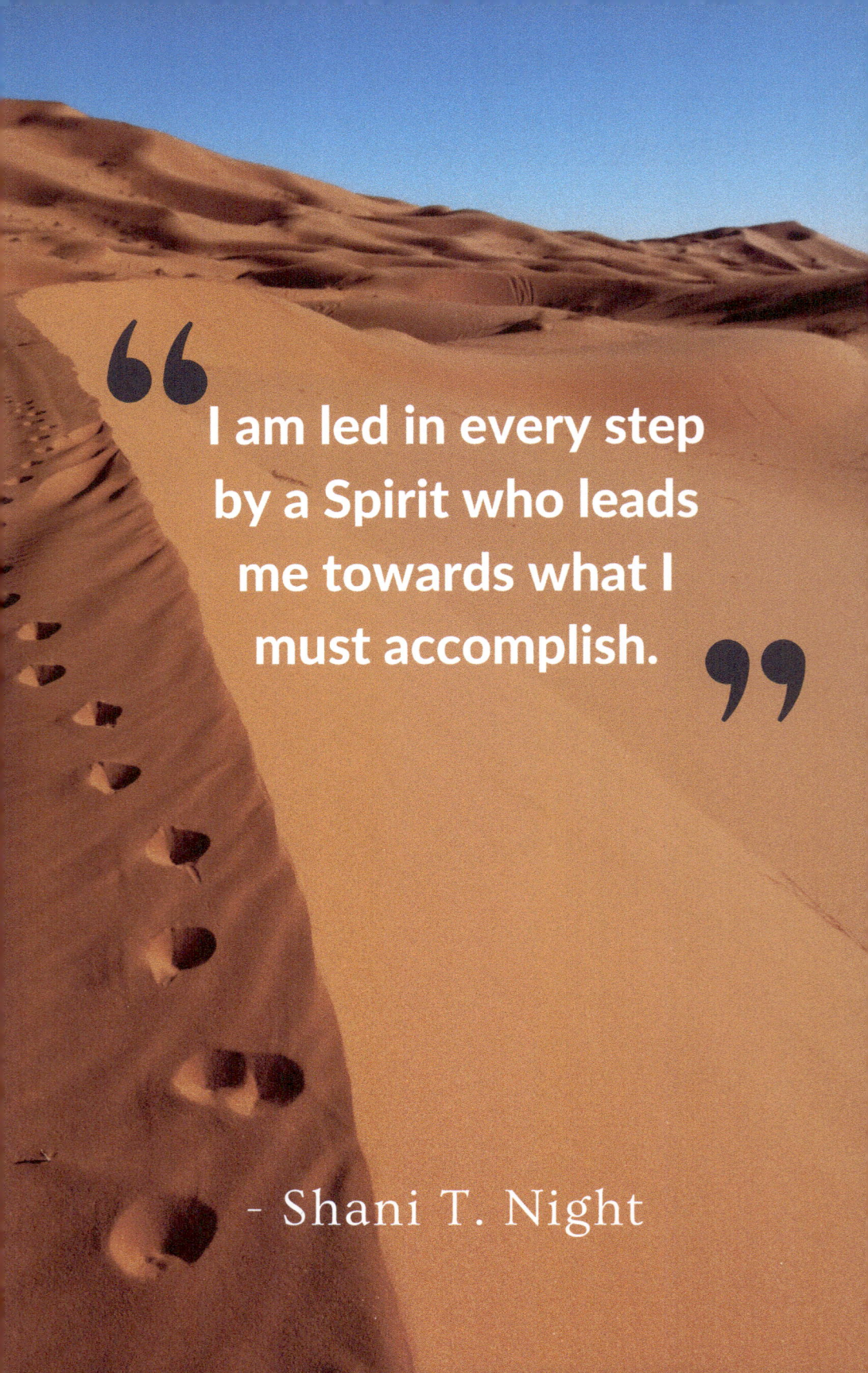

"I am led in every step by a Spirit who leads me towards what I must accomplish."

- Shani T. Night

Good Morning Sunshine

(I always welcome sunshine into my day, first thing in the morning: so welcome sunshine and an open heart to declutter your mind. Continue to do this each day. Share thoughts on how you feel about doing this below.)

Monthly
DECLUTTER YOUR MIND

SET ASPIRATIONS

Think about your aspirations and write them down. Aspirations are more future-focused, like your dreams, hopes, and ambitions.

IDENTIFY YOUR ANEW

Is there anything you did not get accomplished that you set out for yesterday, last week, last month, or last year?

RECOGNIZE - YOU NEED PEACE

Let go of what is not allowing you to have peace. Identify those things and then identify what brings you peace.

SET GOALS

If you don't have a list, identify one goal. Remember, goals are more short-term focused and usually have actions that follow them.

IDENTIFY YOUR INTENTIONS

Are your intentions to be kind and loving?

WELCOME CHANGE - IDENTIFY WHAT YOU CAN DO BETTER

Identify what you need to change in your life or what you want to change.

GRATITUDE REFLECTION - WHAT ARE YOU GRATEFUL FOR AND WHY?

Write it down and reflect on why you feel grateful.

Positive Thoughts

(Thinking positive starts with you; identify what makes you happy and stay positive.)

Weekly Intentions

IDENTIFY YOUR INTENTIONS FOR THE WEEK.

CHANGE
Change is hard, and recognizing change and implementing it is even more challenging, but if you stay positive and focus on being a better you, it will pay off.

ELIMINATE NEGATIVITY AROUND YOU
people/habits/interactions

IDENTIFY WHAT YOU NEED TO WORK ON
Is there anything you did not get accomplished?

LIST THREE THINGS YOU ARE GRATEFUL FOR.
They can be big or small, specific or general. Focus on the positive feelings associated with each. Approach the gratitude exercise with intention.

WELCOME POSITIVE THOUGHTS
Don't forget to welcome sunshine into your day first thing in the morning: welcome sunshine and an open heart to declutter your mind. Continue to do this each day. Share thoughts on how you feel about doing this on the next page.

Intentionally Positive

Positive Thoughts

(Thinking positive starts with you; identify what makes you happy and stay positive.)

WEEKLY PLANNER

MONDAY

TUESDAY

WEDNESDAY

THURSDAY

FRIDAY

SATURDAY

SUNDAY

WEEK OF _____

GOALS

TO DO LIST

PRIORITIES

WEEKLY PLANNER

Monday

Tuesday

Wednesday

Thursday

Friday

Saturday/Sunday

Weekly Notes

to do today

DATE _____

1. _____ ☐
2. _____ ☐
3. _____ ☐
4. _____ ☐
5. _____ ☐
6. _____ ☐
7. _____ ☐
8. _____ ☐
9. _____ ☐
10. _____ ☐

note for today

Weekly Successes

IDENTIFY WHAT SUCCESS LOOKS LIKE TO YOU AND YOU ALONE. **(Don't try to match someone else's success)**

REFLECT

RECOGNIZE THE POSITIVE STEPS YOU'VE TAKEN THIS WEEK TO BE POSITIVE AND DECLUTTER YOUR MIND. **(Take a moment to applaud yourself for taking the necessary steps to start a more positive life.)**

LIST ONE NEGATIVE THING YOU DISCOVERED AROUND YOU. **(people/habits/interactions)** WHAT DID YOU DO ABOUT IT?

WHAT DID YOU DISCOVER ABOUT YOURSELF THIS WEEK?

DID YOU WELCOME CHANGE? WHAT DID YOU CHANGE?

WHAT ARE THREE RECENT ACCOMPLISHMENTS THAT YOU ARE PROUD OF, AND WHAT LESSONS DID YOU DISCOVER IN THE PROCESS?

Intentionally Positive

Weekly Takeaways

NOTE TO SELF

"

I have endless talents
that I will begin to
nourish and use today.

— Shani T. Night

Positive Thoughts

(Thinking positive starts with you; identify what makes you happy and stay positive.)

Weekly Intentions

IDENTIFY YOUR INTENTIONS FOR THE WEEK.

CHANGE
Change is hard, and recognizing change and implementing it is even more challenging, but if you stay positive and focus on being a better you, it will pay off.

ELIMINATE NEGATIVITY AROUND YOU
people/habits/interactions

IDENTIFY WHAT YOU NEED TO WORK ON
Is there anything you did not get accomplished?

LIST THREE THINGS YOU ARE GRATEFUL FOR.
They can be big or small, specific or general. Focus on the positive feelings associated with each. Approach the gratitude exercise with intention.

WELCOME POSITIVE THOUGHTS
Don't forget to welcome sunshine into your day first thing in the morning: welcome sunshine and an open heart to declutter your mind. Continue to do this each day. Share thoughts on how you feel about doing this on the next page.

Intentionally Positive

Positive Thoughts

(Thinking positive starts with you; identify what makes you happy and stay positive.)

WEEKLY PLANNER

WEEK OF _____

MONDAY

TUESDAY

WEDNESDAY

THURSDAY

FRIDAY

SATURDAY

SUNDAY

GOALS

_____

_____

_____

_____

_____

TO DO LIST

_____

_____

_____

_____

_____

_____

_____

PRIORITIES

WEEKLY PLANNER

Monday

Tuesday

Wednesday

Thursday

Friday

Saturday/Sunday

Weekly Notes

to do today

DATE ....

1 _____ ☐

2 _____ ☐

3 _____ ☐

4 _____ ☐

5 _____ ☐

6 _____ ☐

7 _____ ☐

8 _____ ☐

9 _____ ☐

10 _____ ☐

note for today

Weekly Successes

IDENTIFY WHAT SUCCESS LOOKS LIKE TO YOU AND YOU ALONE. **(Don't try to match someone else's success)**

REFLECT

RECOGNIZE THE POSITIVE STEPS YOU'VE TAKEN THIS WEEK TO BE POSITIVE AND DECLUTTER YOUR MIND. **(Take a moment to applaud yourself for taking the necessary steps to start a more positive life.)**

LIST ONE NEGATIVE THING YOU DISCOVERED AROUND YOU. **(people/habits/interactions)** WHAT DID YOU DO ABOUT IT?

WHAT DID YOU DISCOVER ABOUT YOURSELF THIS WEEK?

DID YOU WELCOME CHANGE? WHAT DID YOU CHANGE?

WHAT ARE THREE RECENT ACCOMPLISHMENTS THAT YOU ARE PROUD OF, AND WHAT LESSONS DID YOU DISCOVER IN THE PROCESS?

Intentionally Positive

Weekly Takeaways

NOTE TO SELF

" I have the qualities needed to be highly successful. "

Shani T. Night

Positive Thoughts

(Thinking positive starts with you; identify what makes you happy and stay positive.)

Weekly Intentions

IDENTIFY YOUR INTENTIONS FOR THE WEEK.

CHANGE
Change is hard, and recognizing change and implementing it is even more challenging, but if you stay positive and focus on being a better you, it will pay off.

ELIMINATE NEGATIVITY AROUND YOU
people/habits/interactions

IDENTIFY WHAT YOU NEED TO WORK ON
Is there anything you did not get accomplished?

LIST THREE THINGS YOU ARE GRATEFUL FOR.
They can be big or small, specific or general. Focus on the positive feelings associated with each. Approach the gratitude exercise with intention.

WELCOME POSITIVE THOUGHTS
Don't forget to welcome sunshine into your day first thing in the morning: welcome sunshine and an open heart to declutter your mind. Continue to do this each day. Share thoughts on how you feel about doing this on the next page.

Intentionally Positive

Positive Thoughts

(Thinking positive starts with you; identify what makes you happy and stay positive.)

WEEKLY PLANNER

WEEK OF _____

MONDAY

TUESDAY

WEDNESDAY

THURSDAY

FRIDAY

SATURDAY

SUNDAY

GOALS

TO DO LIST

PRIORITIES

WEEKLY PLANNER

Monday

Tuesday

Wednesday

Thursday

Friday

Saturday/Sunday

Weekly Notes

to do today

DATE ....

1. _____ ☐
2. _____ ☐
3. _____ ☐
4. _____ ☐
5. _____ ☐
6. _____ ☐
7. _____ ☐
8. _____ ☐
9. _____ ☐
10. _____ ☐

note for today

Weekly Successes

IDENTIFY WHAT SUCCESS LOOKS LIKE TO YOU AND YOU ALONE. **(Don't try to match someone else's success)**

REFLECT

RECOGNIZE THE POSITIVE STEPS YOU'VE TAKEN THIS WEEK TO BE POSITIVE AND DECLUTTER YOUR MIND. **(Take a moment to applaud yourself for taking the necessary steps to start a more positive life.)**

LIST ONE NEGATIVE THING YOU DISCOVERED AROUND YOU. **(people/habits/interactions)** WHAT DID YOU DO ABOUT IT?

WHAT DID YOU DISCOVER ABOUT YOURSELF THIS WEEK?

DID YOU WELCOME CHANGE? WHAT DID YOU CHANGE?

WHAT ARE THREE RECENT ACCOMPLISHMENTS THAT YOU ARE PROUD OF, AND WHAT LESSONS DID YOU DISCOVER IN THE PROCESS?

Weekly Takeaways

NOTE TO SELF

" The universe supports my efforts; my dreams manifest into reality before my eyes. "

– Shani T. Night

Positive Thoughts

(Thinking positive starts with you; identify what makes you happy and stay positive.)

Weekly Intentions

IDENTIFY YOUR INTENTIONS FOR THE WEEK.

CHANGE
Change is hard, and recognizing change and implementing it is even more challenging, but if you stay positive and focus on being a better you, it will pay off.

ELIMINATE NEGATIVITY AROUND YOU
people/habits/interactions

IDENTIFY WHAT YOU NEED TO WORK ON
Is there anything you did not get accomplished?

LIST THREE THINGS YOU ARE GRATEFUL FOR.
They can be big or small, specific or general. Focus on the positive feelings associated with each. Approach the gratitude exercise with intention.

WELCOME POSITIVE THOUGHTS
Don't forget to welcome sunshine into your day first thing in the morning: welcome sunshine and an open heart to declutter your mind. Continue to do this each day. Share thoughts on how you feel about doing this on the next page.

Intentionally Positive

Positive Thoughts

(Thinking positive starts with you; identify what makes you happy and stay positive.)

WEEKLY PLANNER

MONDAY

TUESDAY

WEDNESDAY

THURSDAY

FRIDAY

SATURDAY

SUNDAY

WEEK OF _____

GOALS

_____

_____

_____

_____

_____

TO DO LIST

_____

_____

_____

_____

_____

_____

_____

PRIORITIES

WEEKLY PLANNER

Monday

Tuesday

Wednesday

Thursday

Friday

Saturday/Sunday

Weekly Notes

to do today

DATE ....

1 _____ ☐

2 _____ ☐

3 _____ ☐

4 _____ ☐

5 _____ ☐

6 _____ ☐

7 _____ ☐

8 _____ ☐

9 _____ ☐

10 _____ ☐

note for today

Weekly Successes

IDENTIFY WHAT SUCCESS LOOKS LIKE TO YOU AND YOU ALONE. **(Don't try to match someone else's success)**

REFLECT

RECOGNIZE THE POSITIVE STEPS YOU'VE TAKEN THIS WEEK TO BE POSITIVE AND DECLUTTER YOUR MIND. **(Take a moment to applaud yourself for taking the necessary steps to start a more positive life.)**

LIST ONE NEGATIVE THING YOU DISCOVERED AROUND YOU. **(people/habits/interactions)** WHAT DID YOU DO ABOUT IT?

WHAT DID YOU DISCOVER ABOUT YOURSELF THIS WEEK?

DID YOU WELCOME CHANGE? WHAT DID YOU CHANGE?

WHAT ARE THREE RECENT ACCOMPLISHMENTS THAT YOU ARE PROUD OF, AND WHAT LESSONS DID YOU DISCOVER IN THE PROCESS?

Intentionally Positive

Weekly Takeaways

NOTE TO SELF

Next Month

"
Somehow the universe will find you to fulfill your part!
"

WELCOMING THE NEXT
MONTH WITH OPEN ARMS!
- Shani T. Night

Next Steps

"
My future is the positive projection of what I speak into existence now.

— Shani T. Night

Good Morning Sunshine

(I always welcome sunshine into my day, first thing in the morning: so welcome sunshine and an open heart to declutter your mind. Continue to do this each day. Share thoughts on how you feel about doing this below.)

Monthly
DECLUTTER YOUR MIND

SET ASPIRATIONS

Think about your aspirations and write them down. Aspirations are more future-focused, like your dreams, hopes, and ambitions.

IDENTIFY YOUR ANEW

Is there anything you did not get accomplished that you set out for yesterday, last week, last month, or last year?

RECOGNIZE - YOU NEED PEACE

Let go of what is not allowing you to have peace. Identify those things and then identify what brings you peace.

SET GOALS

If you don't have a list, identify one goal. Remember, goals are more short-term focused and usually have actions that follow them.

IDENTIFY YOUR INTENTIONS

Are your intentions to be kind and loving?

WELCOME CHANGE - IDENTIFY WHAT YOU CAN DO BETTER

Identify what you need to change in your life or what you want to change.

GRATITUDE REFLECTION - WHAT ARE YOU GRATEFUL FOR AND WHY?

Write it down and reflect on why you feel grateful.

Positive Thoughts

(Thinking positive starts with you; identify what makes you happy and stay positive.)

Weekly Intentions

IDENTIFY YOUR INTENTIONS FOR THE WEEK.

CHANGE
Change is hard, and recognizing change and implementing it is even more challenging, but if you stay positive and focus on being a better you, it will pay off.

ELIMINATE NEGATIVITY AROUND YOU
people/habits/interactions

IDENTIFY WHAT YOU NEED TO WORK ON
Is there anything you did not get accomplished?

LIST THREE THINGS YOU ARE GRATEFUL FOR.
They can be big or small, specific or general. Focus on the positive feelings associated with each. Approach the gratitude exercise with intention.

WELCOME POSITIVE THOUGHTS
Don't forget to welcome sunshine into your day first thing in the morning: welcome sunshine and an open heart to declutter your mind. Continue to do this each day. Share thoughts on how you feel about doing this on the next page.

Intentionally Positive

Positive Thoughts

(Thinking positive starts with you; identify what makes you happy and stay positive.)

WEEKLY PLANNER

WEEK OF _____

MONDAY

TUESDAY

WEDNESDAY

THURSDAY

FRIDAY

SATURDAY

SUNDAY

GOALS

_____

_____

_____

_____

_____

TO DO LIST

_____

_____

_____

_____

_____

_____

_____

PRIORITIES

WEEKLY PLANNER

Monday

Tuesday

Wednesday

Thursday

Friday

Saturday/Sunday

Weekly Notes

to do today

DATE ....

1 _____ ☐

2 _____ ☐

3 _____ ☐

4 _____ ☐

5 _____ ☐

6 _____ ☐

7 _____ ☐

8 _____ ☐

9 _____ ☐

10 _____ ☐

note for today

Weekly Successes

IDENTIFY WHAT SUCCESS LOOKS LIKE TO YOU AND YOU ALONE. **(Don't try to match someone else's success)**

REFLECT

RECOGNIZE THE POSITIVE STEPS YOU'VE TAKEN THIS WEEK TO BE POSITIVE AND DECLUTTER YOUR MIND. **(Take a moment to applaud yourself for taking the necessary steps to start a more positive life.)**

LIST ONE NEGATIVE THING YOU DISCOVERED AROUND YOU. **(people/habits/interactions)** WHAT DID YOU DO ABOUT IT?

WHAT DID YOU DISCOVER ABOUT YOURSELF THIS WEEK?

DID YOU WELCOME CHANGE? WHAT DID YOU CHANGE?

WHAT ARE THREE RECENT ACCOMPLISHMENTS THAT YOU ARE PROUD OF, AND WHAT LESSONS DID YOU DISCOVER IN THE PROCESS?

Intentionally Positive

Weekly Takeaways

NOTE TO SELF

Positive Thoughts

(Thinking positive starts with you; identify what makes you
happy and stay positive.)

Weekly Intentions

IDENTIFY YOUR INTENTIONS FOR THE WEEK.

CHANGE

Change is hard, and recognizing change and implementing it is even more challenging, but if you stay positive and focus on being a better you, it will pay off.

ELIMINATE NEGATIVITY AROUND YOU

people/habits/interactions

IDENTIFY WHAT YOU NEED TO WORK ON

Is there anything you did not get accomplished?

LIST THREE THINGS YOU ARE GRATEFUL FOR.

They can be big or small, specific or general. Focus on the positive feelings associated with each. Approach the gratitude exercise with intention.

WELCOME POSITIVE THOUGHTS

Don't forget to welcome sunshine into your day first thing in the morning: welcome sunshine and an open heart to declutter your mind. Continue to do this each day. Share thoughts on how you feel about doing this on the next page.

Intentionally Positive

Positive Thoughts

(Thinking positive starts with you; identify what makes you happy and stay positive.)

WEEKLY PLANNER

MONDAY

TUESDAY

WEDNESDAY

THURSDAY

FRIDAY

SATURDAY

SUNDAY

WEEK OF _____

GOALS

_____

_____

_____

_____

_____

TO DO LIST

_____

_____

_____

_____

_____

_____

_____

PRIORITIES

WEEKLY PLANNER

Monday

Tuesday

Wednesday

Thursday

Friday

Saturday/Sunday

Weekly Notes

to do today

DATE ....

1 _____ ☐

2 _____ ☐

3 _____ ☐

4 _____ ☐

5 _____ ☐

6 _____ ☐

7 _____ ☐

8 _____ ☐

9 _____ ☐

10 _____ ☐

note for today

Weekly Successes

IDENTIFY WHAT SUCCESS LOOKS LIKE TO YOU AND YOU ALONE. **(Don't try to match someone else's success)**

REFLECT

RECOGNIZE THE POSITIVE STEPS YOU'VE TAKEN THIS WEEK TO BE POSITIVE AND DECLUTTER YOUR MIND. **(Take a moment to applaud yourself for taking the necessary steps to start a more positive life.)**

LIST ONE NEGATIVE THING YOU DISCOVERED AROUND YOU. **(people/habits/interactions)** WHAT DID YOU DO ABOUT IT?

WHAT DID YOU DISCOVER ABOUT YOURSELF THIS WEEK?

DID YOU WELCOME CHANGE? WHAT DID YOU CHANGE?

WHAT ARE THREE RECENT ACCOMPLISHMENTS THAT YOU ARE PROUD OF, AND WHAT LESSONS DID YOU DISCOVER IN THE PROCESS?

Weekly Takeaways

NOTE TO SELF

I am focused on the present.

Shani T. Night

Positive Thoughts

(Thinking positive starts with you; identify what makes you happy and stay positive.)

Weekly Intentions

IDENTIFY YOUR INTENTIONS FOR THE WEEK.

CHANGE
Change is hard, and recognizing change and implementing it is even more challenging, but if you stay positive and focus on being a better you, it will pay off.

ELIMINATE NEGATIVITY AROUND YOU
people/habits/interactions

IDENTIFY WHAT YOU NEED TO WORK ON
Is there anything you did not get accomplished?

LIST THREE THINGS YOU ARE GRATEFUL FOR.
They can be big or small, specific or general. Focus on the positive feelings associated with each. Approach the gratitude exercise with intention.

WELCOME POSITIVE THOUGHTS
Don't forget to welcome sunshine into your day first thing in the morning: welcome sunshine and an open heart to declutter your mind. Continue to do this each day. Share thoughts on how you feel about doing this on the next page.

Intentionally Positive

Positive Thoughts

(Thinking positive starts with you; identify what makes you happy and stay positive.)

WEEKLY PLANNER

WEEK OF _____

MONDAY

TUESDAY

WEDNESDAY

THURSDAY

FRIDAY

SATURDAY

SUNDAY

GOALS

TO DO LIST

PRIORITIES

WEEKLY PLANNER

Monday

Tuesday

Wednesday

Thursday

Friday

Saturday/Sunday

Weekly Notes

to do today

DATE _____

1 _____ ☐

2 _____ ☐

3 _____ ☐

4 _____ ☐

5 _____ ☐

6 _____ ☐

7 _____ ☐

8 _____ ☐

9 _____ ☐

10 _____ ☐

note for today

Weekly Successes

IDENTIFY WHAT SUCCESS LOOKS LIKE TO YOU AND YOU ALONE. **(Don't try to match someone else's success)**

REFLECT

RECOGNIZE THE POSITIVE STEPS YOU'VE TAKEN THIS WEEK TO BE POSITIVE AND DECLUTTER YOUR MIND. **(Take a moment to applaud yourself for taking the necessary steps to start a more positive life.)**

LIST ONE NEGATIVE THING YOU DISCOVERED AROUND YOU. **(people/habits/interactions)** WHAT DID YOU DO ABOUT IT?

WHAT DID YOU DISCOVER ABOUT YOURSELF THIS WEEK?

DID YOU WELCOME CHANGE? WHAT DID YOU CHANGE?

WHAT ARE THREE RECENT ACCOMPLISHMENTS THAT YOU ARE PROUD OF, AND WHAT LESSONS DID YOU DISCOVER IN THE PROCESS?

Intentionally Positive

Weekly Takeaways

NOTE TO SELF

"I wake up today with love in my heart, strength in my soul, and clarity in my mind."

– Shani T. Night

Positive Thoughts

(Thinking positive starts with you; identify what makes you happy and stay positive.)

Weekly Intentions

IDENTIFY YOUR INTENTIONS FOR THE WEEK.

CHANGE
Change is hard, and recognizing change and implementing it is even more challenging, but if you stay positive and focus on being a better you, it will pay off.

ELIMINATE NEGATIVITY AROUND YOU
people/habits/interactions

IDENTIFY WHAT YOU NEED TO WORK ON
Is there anything you did not get accomplished?

LIST THREE THINGS YOU ARE GRATEFUL FOR.
They can be big or small, specific or general. Focus on the positive feelings associated with each. Approach the gratitude exercise with intention.

WELCOME POSITIVE THOUGHTS
Don't forget to welcome sunshine into your day first thing in the morning: welcome sunshine and an open heart to declutter your mind. Continue to do this each day. Share thoughts on how you feel about doing this on the next page.

Intentionally Positive

Positive Thoughts

(Thinking positive starts with you; identify what makes you happy and stay positive.)

WEEKLY PLANNER

MONDAY

TUESDAY

WEDNESDAY

THURSDAY

FRIDAY

SATURDAY

SUNDAY

WEEK OF _____

GOALS

_____

_____

_____

_____

_____

TO DO LIST

_____

_____

_____

_____

_____

_____

_____

PRIORITIES

WEEKLY PLANNER

Monday

Tuesday

Wednesday

Thursday

Friday

Saturday/Sunday

Weekly Notes

to do today

DATE ....

1 _____ ☐

2 _____ ☐

3 _____ ☐

4 _____ ☐

5 _____ ☐

6 _____ ☐

7 _____ ☐

8 _____ ☐

9 _____ ☐

10 _____ ☐

note for today

Weekly Successes

IDENTIFY WHAT SUCCESS LOOKS LIKE TO YOU AND YOU ALONE. **(Don't try to match someone else's success)**

REFLECT

RECOGNIZE THE POSITIVE STEPS YOU'VE TAKEN THIS WEEK TO BE POSITIVE AND DECLUTTER YOUR MIND. **(Take a moment to applaud yourself for taking the necessary steps to start a more positive life.)**

LIST ONE NEGATIVE THING YOU DISCOVERED AROUND YOU. **(people/habits/interactions)** WHAT DID YOU DO ABOUT IT?

WHAT DID YOU DISCOVER ABOUT YOURSELF THIS WEEK?

DID YOU WELCOME CHANGE? WHAT DID YOU CHANGE?

WHAT ARE THREE RECENT ACCOMPLISHMENTS THAT YOU ARE PROUD OF, AND WHAT LESSONS DID YOU DISCOVER IN THE PROCESS?

Intentionally Positive

Weekly Takeaways

NOTE TO SELF

"

I move impediments out of my way; my future is blessed with marvelous things.

- Shani T. Night

Good Morning Sunshine

(I always welcome sunshine into my day, first thing in the morning: so welcome sunshine and an open heart to declutter your mind. Continue to do this each day. Share thoughts on how you feel about doing this below.)

> Love and kindness are the keys to life. Love yourself through the pain and the letdowns. Like all that you do and how you do it. Try to grow and get better each day. #iamwriting to share what I love most.

– Shani T. Night

Positive Thoughts

(Thinking positive starts with you; identify what makes you happy and stay positive.)

Reflection

Date:

BAD HABITS I NEED TO STOP

THINGS I REGRETTED NOT DOING

THINGS I LEARNED THE LAST 3-4 MONTHS

HOW TO BE A BETTER VERSION OF ME

Achievements

Let's take stock of where you are today.....

Today you are thinking positively. You are a positive thinker. You can see both sides of things, negative and positive, and you choose to be positive.

You are more aware of yourself and your thoughts. But, more importantly, you are true to who you are and who you want to be.

You are fearless. You don't fear changes or ups and downs.

You surround yourself with positive people.

You don't let mistakes stand in your way.

You are not easily discouraged.

You are your inspiration.

You engage positively.

You are present.

You are happy.

You are

Intentionally Positive

Next Steps

Don't forget to check out the following:

- Intentionally Positive Path to Positive Change: A Guided Journal for Transformation Vol. I
- Intentionally Positive Continuing the Journey: A Guided Journal for Sustaining Positive Change Vol. II
- Free session with the purchase of this book **(schedule on my website)**

Intentionally Positive Journals and Planners are sold on my website:
www.shanitnight.com

Important Dates

DATE	EVENT	NOTES

Take a little time to enjoy the view.

www.ingramcontent.com/pod-product-compliance
Lightning Source LLC
Chambersburg PA
CBHW051308120626
46547CB00015B/2147